Letterland

PICTURE DICTIONARY

Devised and written by Richard Carlisle

Educational Editor: Lyn Wendon

Collins Educational

An imprint of HarperCollinsPublishers

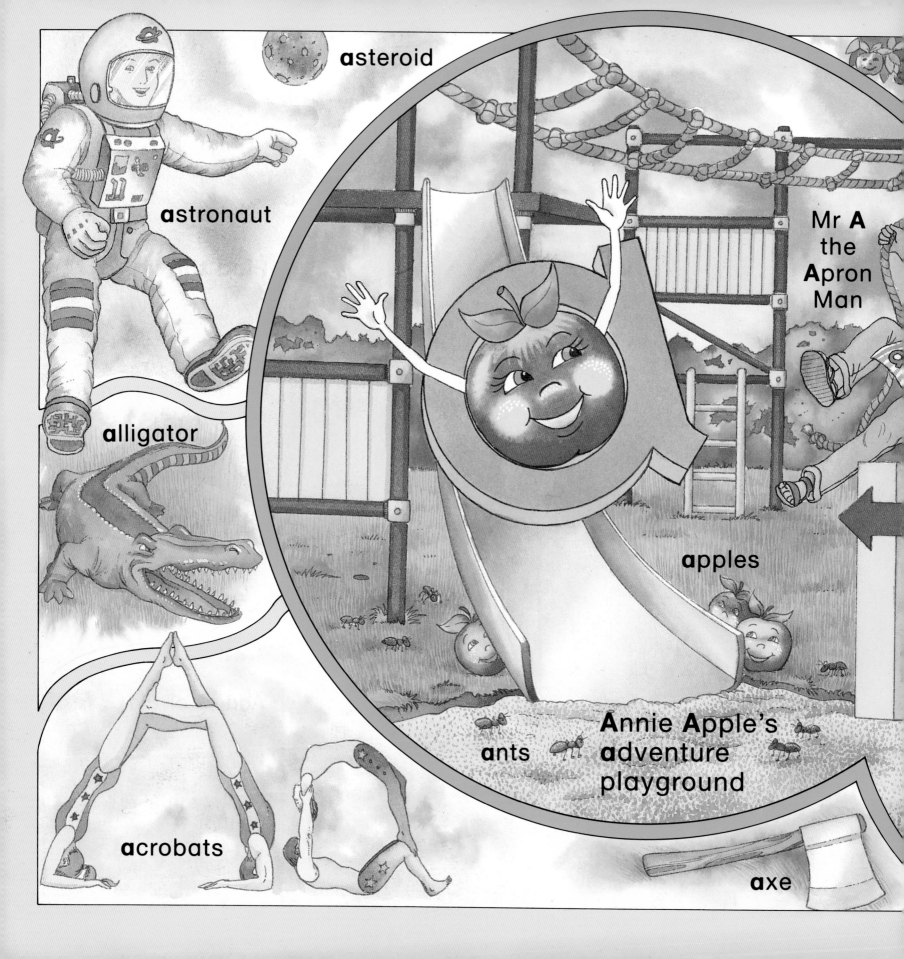

asteroid

astronaut

alligator

acrobats

Mr **A** the **A**pron Man

apples

Annie **A**pple's adventure playground

ants

axe

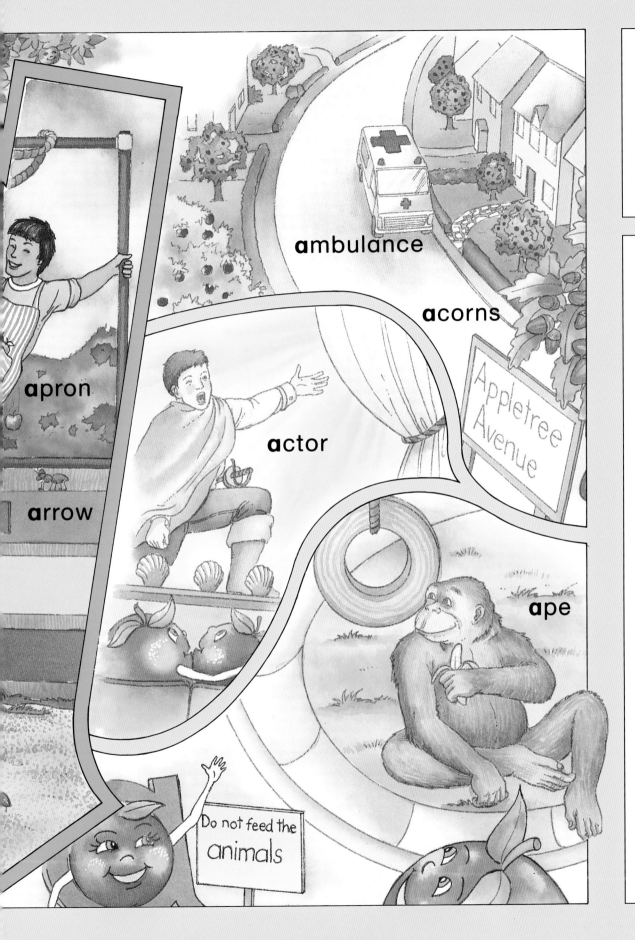

ambulance

acorns

apron

actor

arrow

ape

Appletree Avenue

Do not feed the animals

A a

Find the word

acrobats   apples
actor   Appletree
adventure   arrow
alligator   asteroid
ambulance
animals   astronaut
Annie   Avenue
ants   axe
Apple

Mr **A**
acorns   apron
ape

Activities

Add up all the apples.

Add up all the ants.

Find an angry animal.

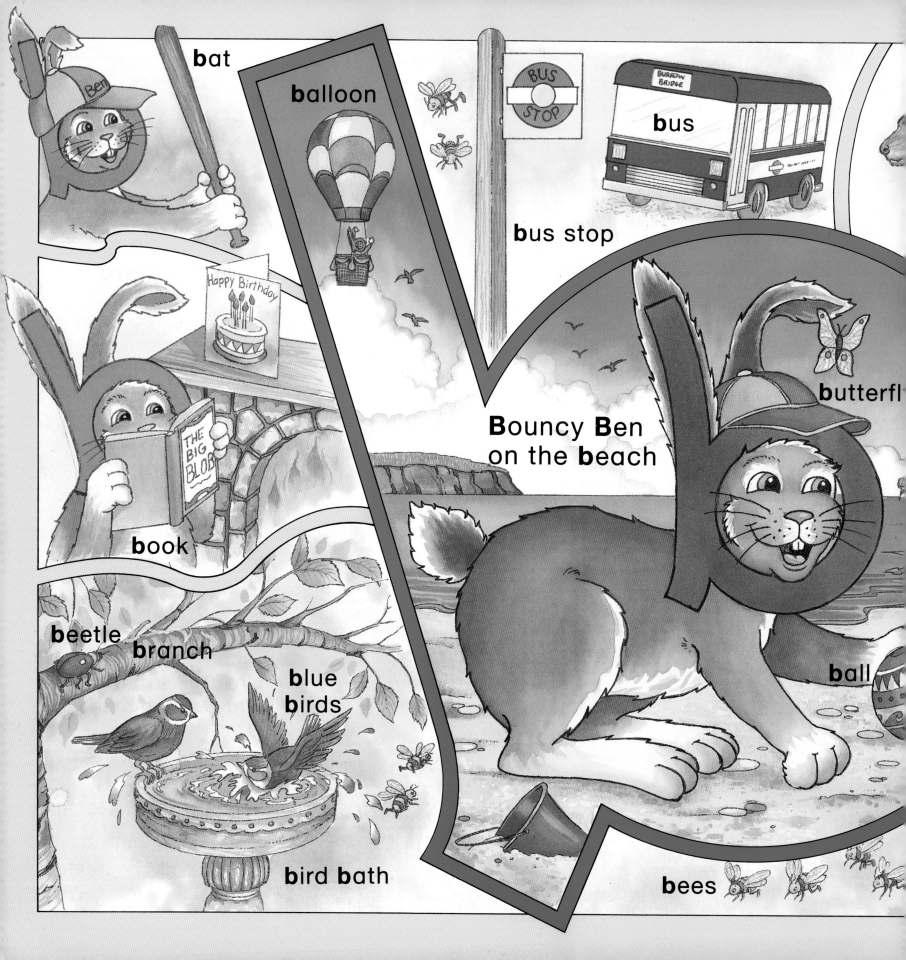

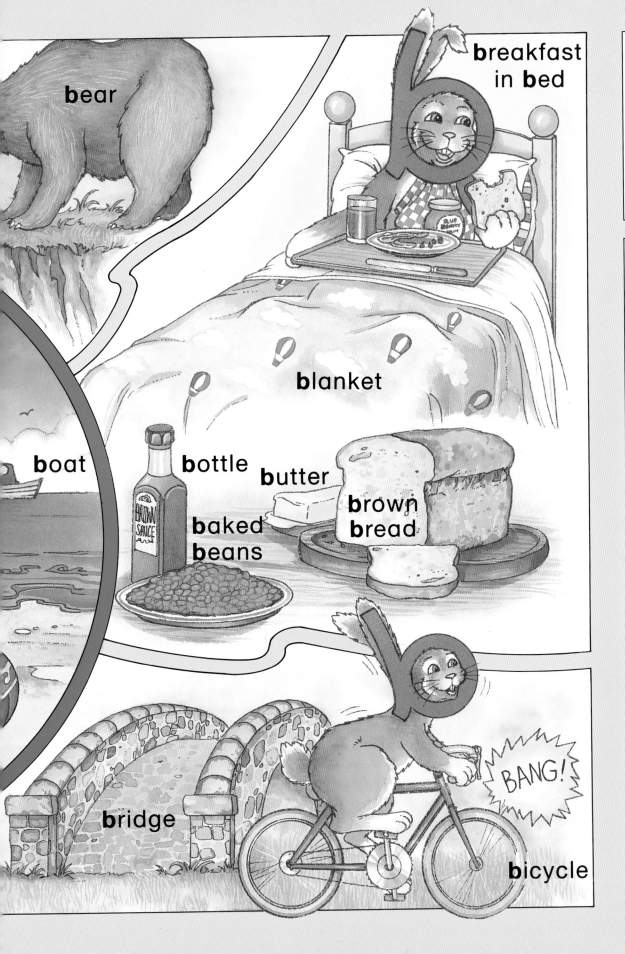

bear

breakfast
in bed

blanket

boat

bottle

butter

baked
beans

brown
bread

bridge

bicycle

Bb

Find the word

baked	Birthday
ball	blanket
balloon	BLOB
BANG!	blue
bat	boat
bath	book
beach	bottle
beans	Bouncy
bear	branch
bed	bread
bees	breakfast
beetle	bridge
Ben	brown
bicycle	bus
BIG	bus stop
bird	butter
birds	butterfly

Activities

Count all the bees.

Find something
buried on the beach.

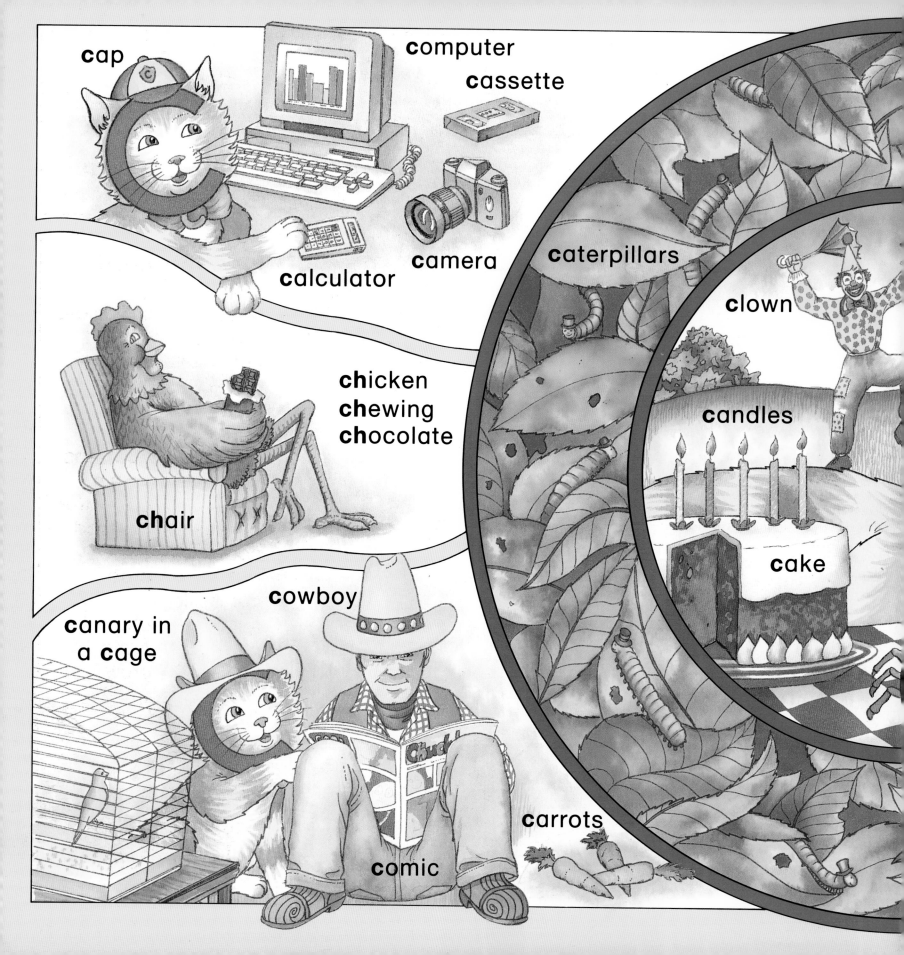

clock covered in cobwebs

crow

Clever Cat's picnic

church

camel

claws

crab

crane

crate

car

Find the word

cage	chocolate
cake	church
calculator	Clever
camel	claws
camera	clock
canary	clown
candles	cobwebs
cap	comic
car	computer
carrots	covered
cassette	cowboy
Cat	crab
caterpillars	
chair	crane
chewing	crate
chicken	crow

Activities

Find all the caterpillars.

Count the candles on Clever Cat's cake.

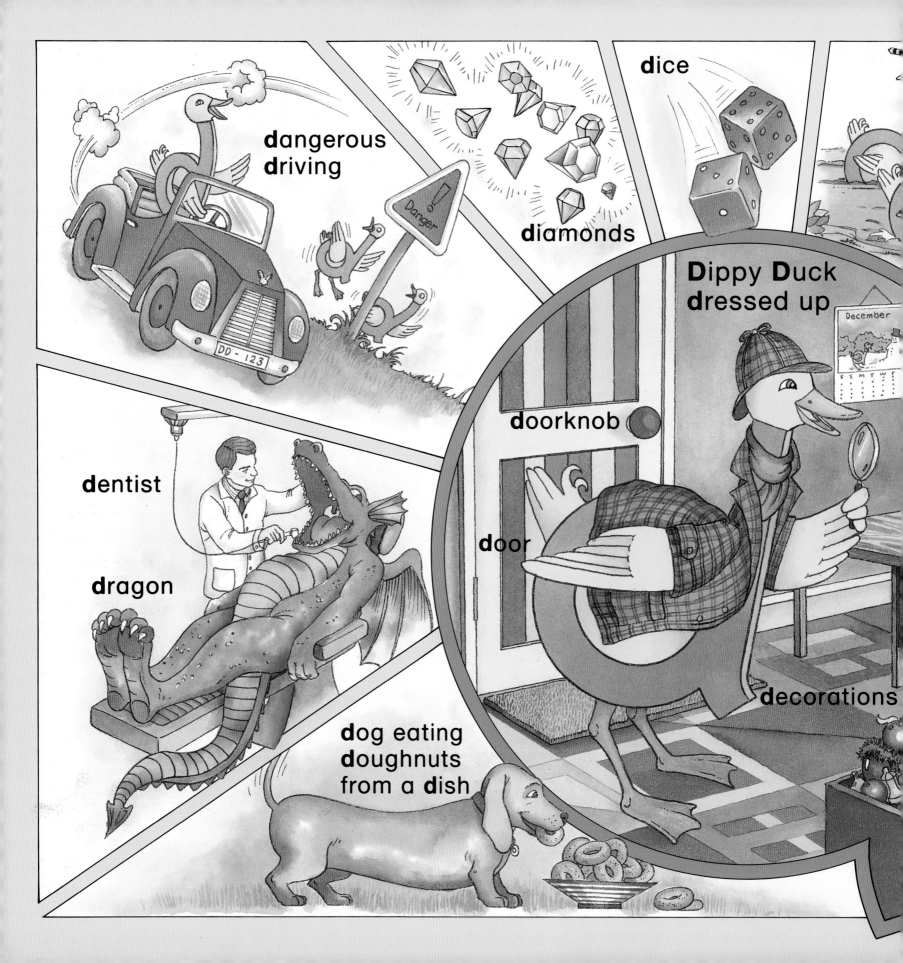

daffodils

dartboard

Doctor in a
deckchair

desk

doll

diving dolphins

drum

drumsticks

Which door is
different?

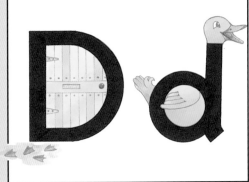

Dd

Find the word

daffodils   DO
Danger!   Doctor
dangerous
dartboard   dog
December   doll
deckchair   dolphins
decorations
dentist   door
desk   doorknob
diamonds   doughnuts
dice   dragon
different   dressed
Dippy   driving
dish   drum
DISTURB   drumsticks
diving   Duck

Activities

Add up the dots on
the dice.

Find the dove.

Count the ducks.

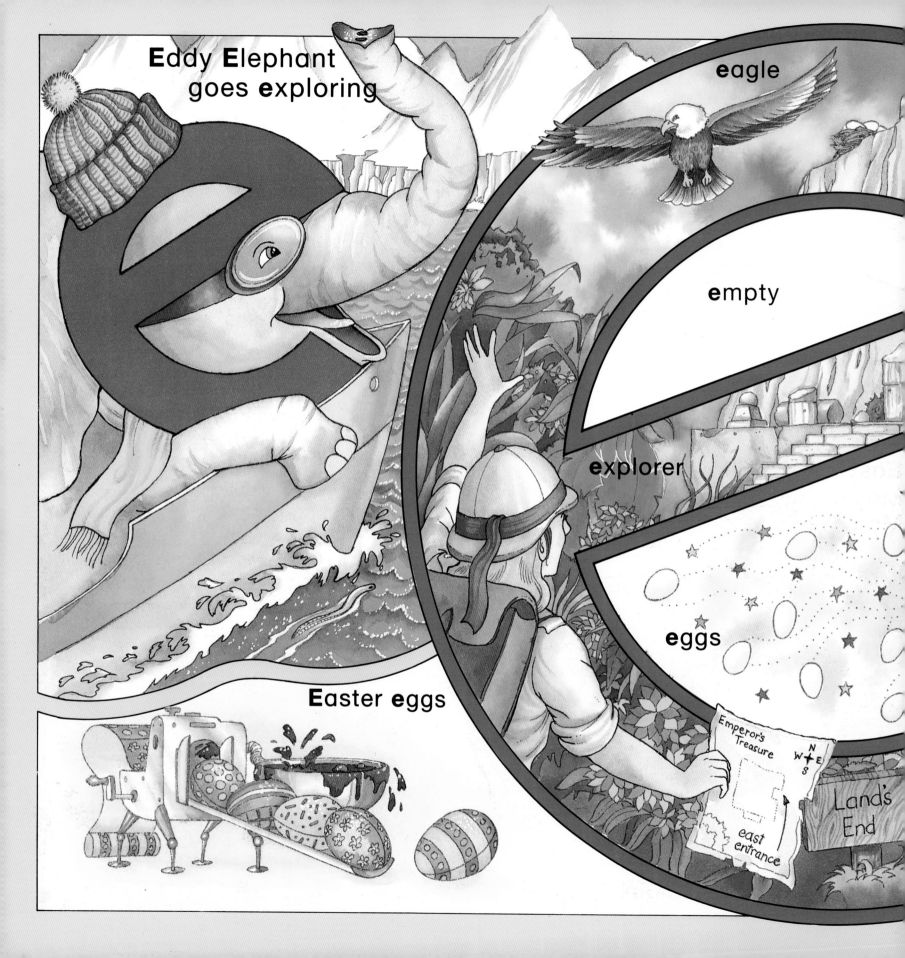

Eddy **E**lephant
goes **e**xploring

eagle

empty

explorer

eggs

Easter **e**ggs

Emperor's Treasure

east entrance

Land's End

envelope

E. Elephant
11 Elmtree Estate
Letterland

escalator

entrance

EXIT

explosion

Mr E the
Easy
Magic
Man

Eddy **E**lephant
eating **e**clairs

E e

Find the word

eclairs	**e**ntrance
Eddy	**e**nvelope
eggs	**e**scalator
Elephant	**E**state
Elm	**E**XIT
Elmtree	**e**xplorer
Emperor	**e**xploring
empty	**e**xplosion
End	

Mr E

eagle	**E**asy
east	**e**ating
Easter	

Activities

Add up all the eggs.

Find whose treasure is on the map.

Find the hidden eel.

Fireworks with Fireman Fred

fireflies in the **f**orest

funny **f**ace on a **f**lag

factory

fence

fields

fox

fern

football

frog

FIRST AID

fifty pence

fork

fire engine

frog

farm

farmer

F f

Find the word

face	Fireworks
factory	FIRST AID
farm	flag
farmer	football
fence	forest
fern	fork
fields	fox
fifty pence	Fred
fire engine	frog
fireflies	funny
Fireman	Fulham

Activities

Count the fireflies.

Count the foxes in the field.

Find a hidden fish.

guitar

goal

gate

grapes

glider

garage

garden

goggles

grass

gloves

game

Golden **G**irl's **g**reenhouse

glass

glasses

gorilla

granny
and
grandad

goat
grazing

goose

ghost

go kart

Find the word

game	**g**oggles
garage	**g**o kart
garden	**G**olden
gate	**g**oose
ghost	**g**orilla
Girl	**g**randad
glass	**g**ranny
glasses	**g**rapes
glider	**g**rass
gloves	**g**razing
goal	**g**reenhouse
goat	**g**uitar

Activities

Count the animals.

Find the grasshopper.

Find the green grapes.

The **H**airy **H**at Man at **h**ome

hatstand

Home Sweet Home

hair

hand

hill

hamburger

honey

hat

hay

horse

holly

HOTEL

helmet

Hilltop Hotel

hippo

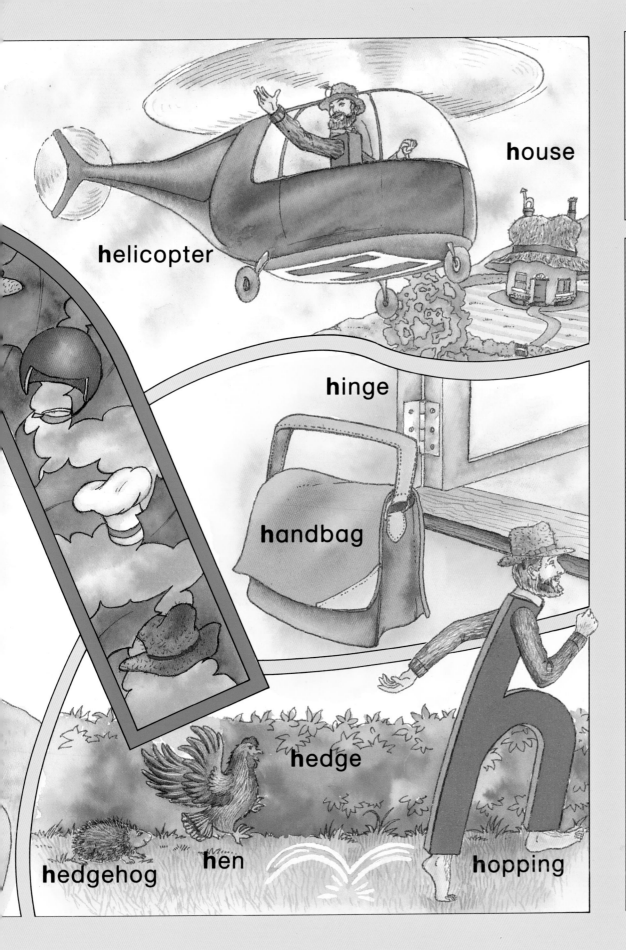

house

helicopter

hinge

handbag

hedge

hedgehog

hen

hopping

Hh

Find the word

hair	**h**ill
Hairy	**H**illtop
hamburger	
hand	**h**inge
handbag	**h**ippo
hat	**h**olly
hatstand	**h**ome
hay	**h**oney
hedge	**h**opping
hedgehog	**h**orse
helicopter	**H**OTEL
helmet	**h**ouse
hen	

Activities

Find the hammer.

Find the hidden hippo.

Count the hats.

Find all the helmets.

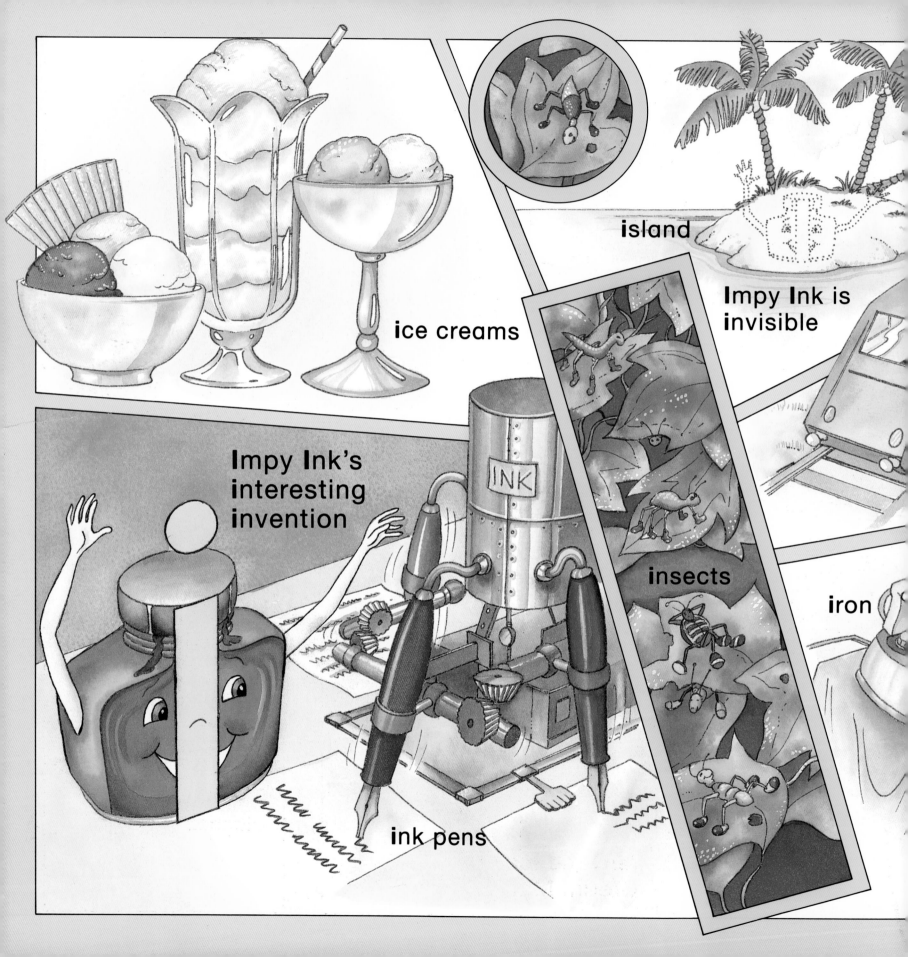

ice creams

island

Impy Ink is invisible

Impy Ink's interesting invention

insects

iron

ink pens

INK

ill

igloo

intercity train

ice skating

invitation

Mr I the Ice Cream Man

Find the word

igloo	interesting
ill	invention
Impy	invisible
Ink	invitation
ink pens	is
insects	
intercity train	

Mr I
ice creams
ice skating
iron
island

Activities

Count the insects.

Count all the ice creams.

Find the invisible islander.

jumping joker

juggling balls

jelly

jacket

jeans

Jumping Jim's
jam machine

judge

jellies

jam
jars

jigsaw

jelly fish

Jumbo **j**et

jewels

jug

jeep

jaguars in the **j**ungle

J j

Find the word

jacket	**j**igsaw
jaguars	**J**im
jam	**j**oke book
jars	**j**oker
jeans	**j**udge
jeep	**j**ug
jellies	**j**uggling
jelly	**J**umbo
jelly fish	**J**umping
jet	**j**umping
jewels	**j**ungle

Activities

Count the juggling balls.

Find the hidden jelly.

Find the jack-in-the-box.

kites

koala

knight
knitting

kennel

Kicking King's
kites

kitchen

kettle

ketchup

key

1 Kilometre to the Kingdom

kittens

kangaroos kissing

Kk

Find the word

kangaroos
kennel
ketchup
kettle
Kevin
key
Kicking
King
kilometre

kingdom
kissing
kitchen
kites
kittens
knight
knitting
koala

Activities

Find two keys.

Count the kittens.

Count the kites.

lemons

lightning

lighthouse

logs

ladder

lamb

lifeboat

light
lunch

lettuce
lemon
lime juice

lesson

Len's
Leeks

lorry

Find the word

ladder	lettuce
Lady	library
lake	lifeboat
lamb	light
Lamp	lighthouse
lawn	lightning
laying	lime
lazy	lion
leaves	logs
Leeks	lorry
lemon	luggage
Len	lunch box
lesson	
LETTERLAND	

Activities

Find the lizard.

Count all the lambs.

Look for a lollipop.

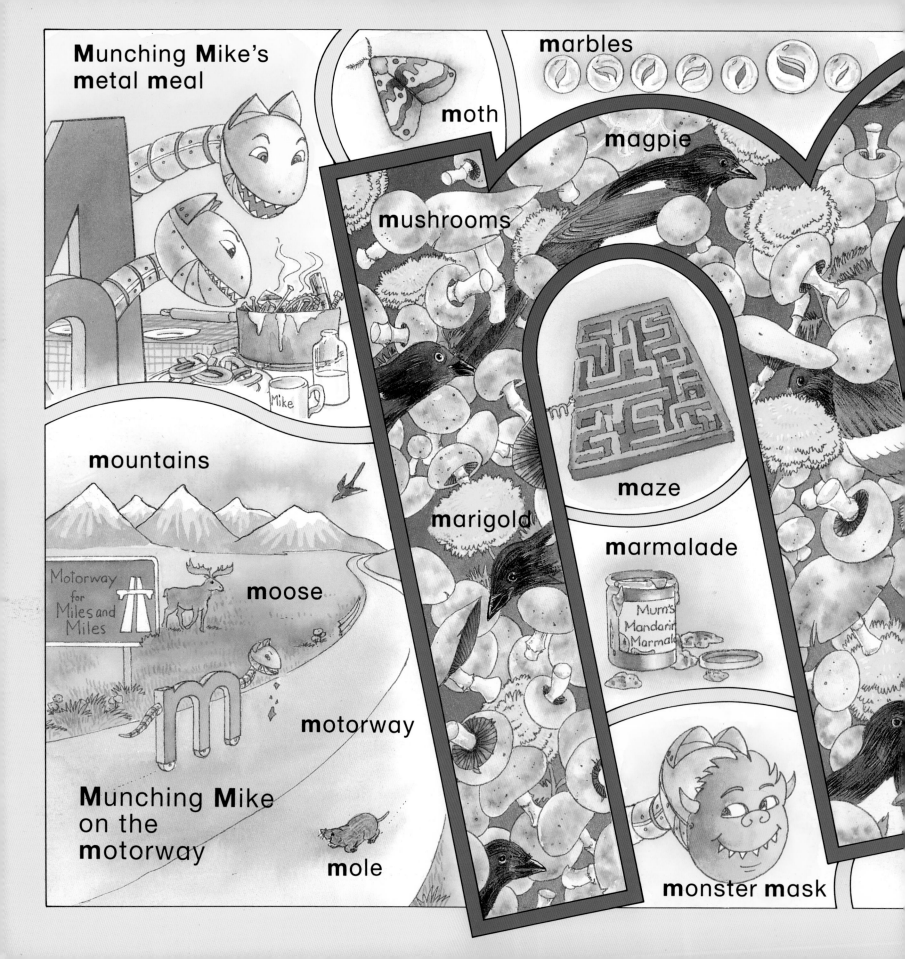

Munching **M**ike's
metal **m**eal

moth

marbles

magpie

mushrooms

mountains

maze

marigold

marmalade

Mum's
Mandarin
Marmalade

moose

Motorway
for
Miles and
Miles

motorway

Munching **M**ike
on the
motorway

mole

monster **m**ask

Mm

map

monkey

magic mirror

model

microphone

music

motorbike

Find the word

magic   model
magpie   mole
Mandarin   monkey
map   monster
marbles   moose
marigold   moth
market   motorbike
marmalade
mask   motorway
maze   mountains
meal   Mum
metal   Munching
microphone
Mike   Museum
Miles   mushrooms
mirror   music
Misty

Activities

Count the magpies.

What is in Munching Mike's meal?

nest

No Entry

No Cycling

Notices

number nine

nightly News 9p

No More Noise say Nick's neighbours

Naughty Nick's newspaper

noisy

neighbours

nails

needle

night

nurse

Find the word

nails	nine
Naughty	No
needle	Noise
neighbours	
nest	noisy
net	Notices
News	number
newspaper	
Nick	nurse
night	nuts
nightly	

Activities

Find the hidden nightingale.

Add up all the nails.

Find the necklaces.

Count all the nests.

oranges

oranges from overseas

one **o**'clock

olives

otter

Oscar **O**range
over the **o**cean

On or
off?

on off

on off

Mr **O**

octopus

office

ostrich

Find the word

octopus	**O**range
off	**o**ranges
office	**O**scar
olives	**o**strich
On	**o**tter

Mr **O**	**o**pen
ocean	**o**ver
o'clock	**o**verseas

Activities

Add up all the oranges.

How many legs on one octopus?

Which orange is the odd one out?

purple paint

playground

pony

pond

Private

picnic

policeman

paper plane

panda

present

Find the word

paint	pig
painting	pirate
palm trees	plane
Pam	playground
panda	policeman
paper	pond
parcels	pony
parrot	Poor
paws	poppies
pears	postbox
pencil	postman
penguins	present
pennies	Private
Peter	puddle
piano	puppet
picnic	purple
picture	

Activities

Find all the presents.

What are the penguins playing?

question mark

The question is... What is is the

quail

quiet please

Quarrelsome **Qu**een's **qu**iet room

robot

run ~ rob return

quiver

quiz

quill

quilt

quarters

quads

ring

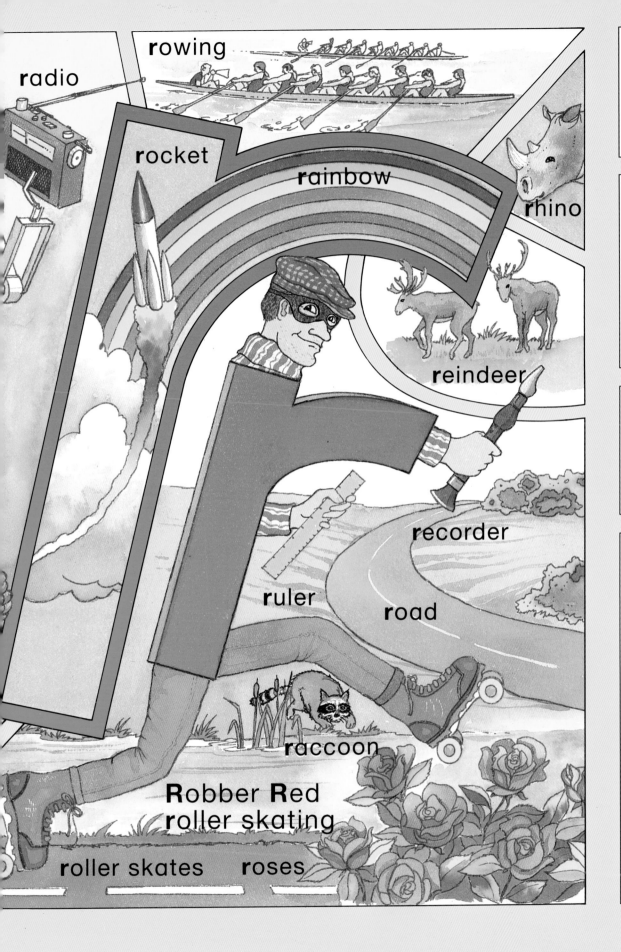

radio

rowing

rocket

rainbow

rhino

reindeer

recorder

ruler

road

raccoon

Robber **R**ed
roller skating

roller skates   **r**oses

Find the word

quads	**qu**iet
quail	**qu**ill
Quarrelsome	**Qu**een
quarters	**qu**ilt
question	**qu**iver

raccoon	**r**ob
radio	**R**obber
rainbow	**r**obot
recorder	**r**ocket
Red	**r**oller skates
reindeer	**r**ope
return	**r**oses
rhino	**r**owing
ring	**r**uler
road	**r**un

Activities

Find the reeds

Count the roses.

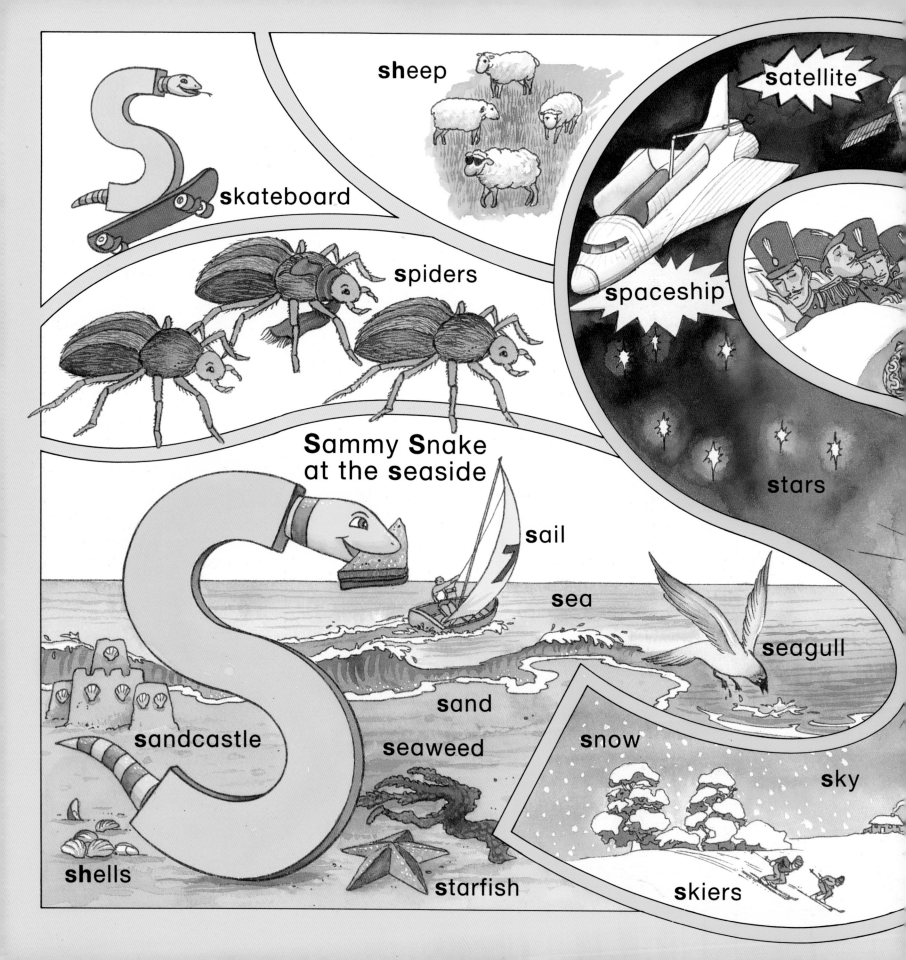

sheep

satellite

skateboard

spiders

spaceship

Sammy **S**nake
at the **s**easide

sail

stars

sea

seagull

sand

sandcastle

seaweed

snow

sky

shells

starfish

skiers

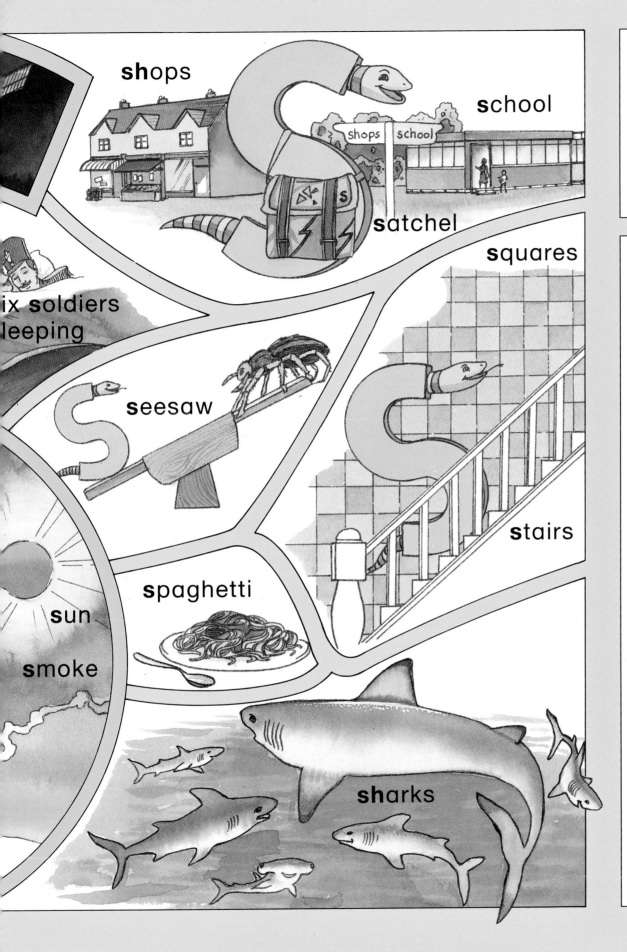

shops

school

satchel

squares

s**ix** **s**oldiers **s**leeping

seesaw

stairs

spaghetti

sun

smoke

sharks

Ss

Find the word

sail	**s**kateboard
Sammy	**s**kiers
sand	**s**ky
sandcastle	**s**leeping
satchel	**s**moke
satellite	**S**nake
school	**s**now
sea	**s**oldiers
seagull	**s**paceship
seaside	**s**paghetti
seaweed	**s**piders
seesaw	**s**quares
sharks	**s**tairs
sheep	**s**tarfish
shells	**s**tars
shops	**s**un
six	**s**word

Activities

Count the sharks.

Find the sword.

Add up all the stars.

tiger

train

two tents

taxi

toothbrush

tissue

tap

toothpaste

towel

typewriter

teddy bear

television

toys

tomatoes

Ticking Tess on the telephone

tape recorder

tortoise

ten tadpoles

trees

teapot

tractor

table

target

Ticking Tom

toadstools

Find the word

table	toadstools
tadpoles	Tom
tap	tomatoes
tape recorder	
target	toothbrush
taxi	toothpaste
teapot	tortoise
teddy bear	
telephone	towel
television	toys
ten	tractor
tents	train
Tess	trees
Ticking	two
tiger	typewriter
tissue	

Activities

Count the tomatoes.

Find three tortoises.

Find the traffic lights.

Find the trampoline.

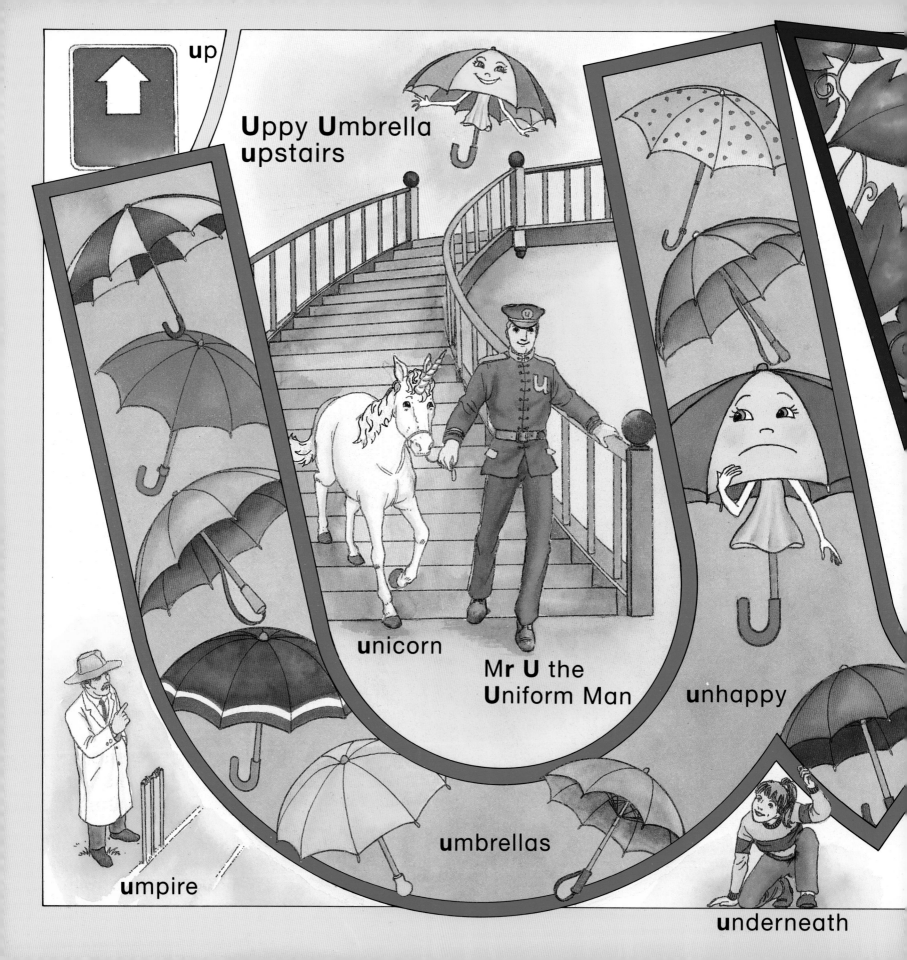

up

Uppy **U**mbrella
upstairs

unicorn

M**r U** the
Uniform Man

unhappy

umbrellas

umpire

underneath

volcano

vulture with a violin

vines

viaduct

Vase of Violets

valley

van

Uu

Find the word

umbrellas	**u**p
umpire	**U**ppy
underneath	**u**pstairs
unhappy	

Mr **U**   **U**niform Man
unicorn

Vv

Find the word

valley	**V**ince
van	**v**ines
Vase	**v**iolets
Vegetables	**v**iolin
Vet	**v**isitors
viaduct	**v**olcano
village	**v**ulture

Activities

Add up the umbrellas.

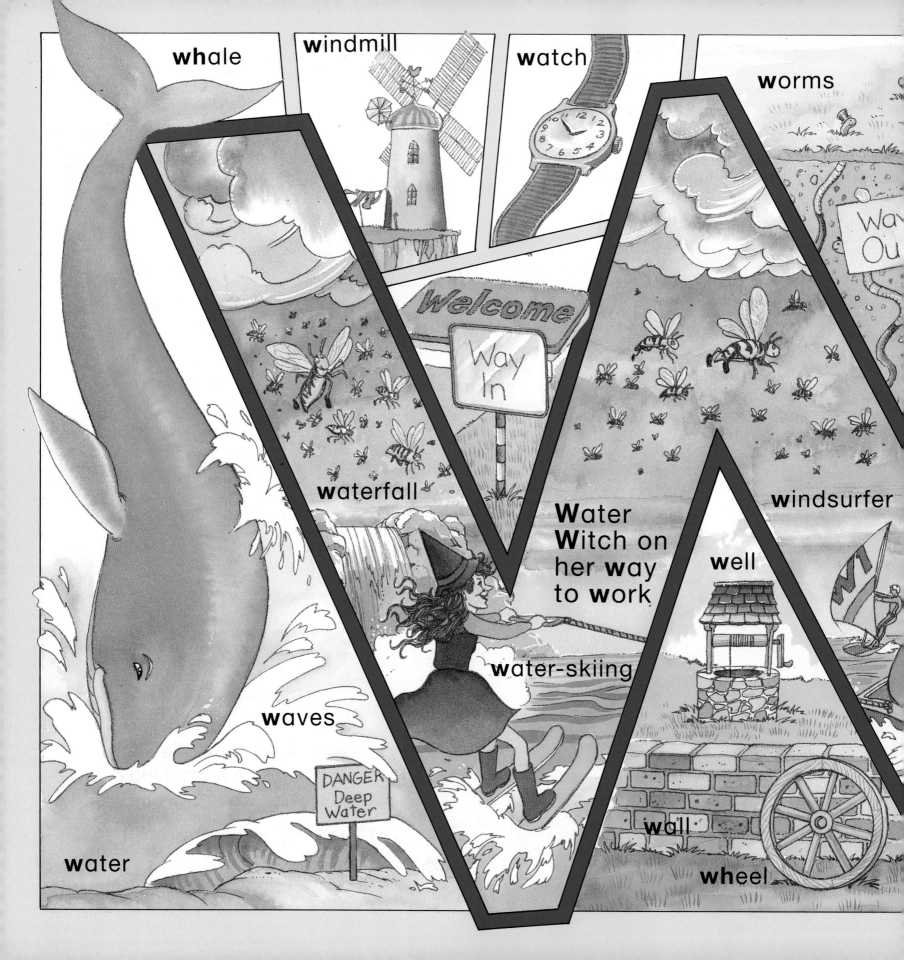

wood

wolf

wasps

walrus

washing machine

Wet Wild
Wash Wash Woollies

wool

wellington boots

Find the word

wall	Wet
walrus	whale
Wash	wheel
washing machine	
wasps	Wild
watch	windmill
Water	windsurfer
waterfall	Witch
water-skiing	
waves	wolf
way	wood
Way In	wool
Way Out	Woollies
Welcome	work
well	worms
wellington boots	

Activities

What is the Water Witch washing?

Who is the wolf waiting for?

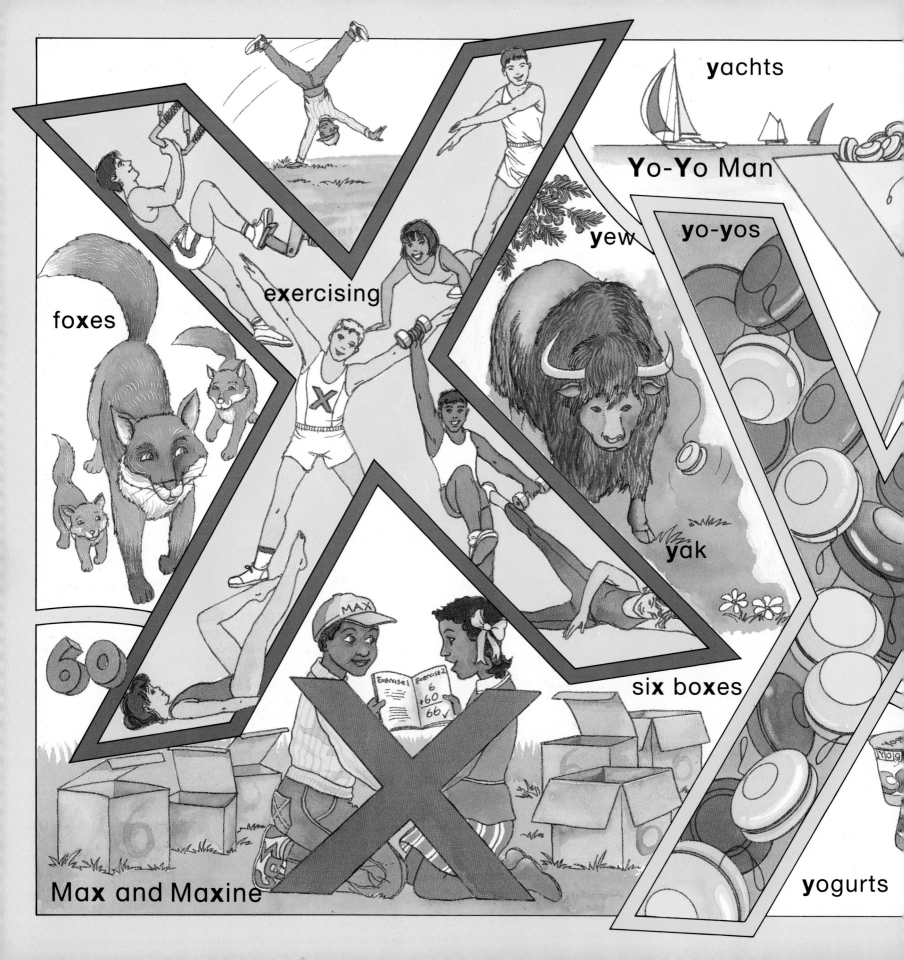

foxes

exercising

Max and Maxine

six boxes

yachts

Yo-Yo Man

yew

yo-yos

yak

yogurts

zoo

Zig
Zag
Zebra

zebra
crossing

zip

Find the word

bo**x**es	Ma**x**
e**x**ercising	Ma**x**ine
fo**x**es	si**x**

yachts	**y**o-**y**os
yak	**y**ogurts
yew	**Y**o-**Y**o Man

Zebra	**z**oo
zebra crossing	
Zig **Z**ag	**Z**OOM!
zip	

six lambs

seven Easter eggs

nine mushrooms

eight apples

ten bouncy balls

This book is dedicated to Alexander Carlisle – R.H.C.

Published by Collins Educational
An imprint of HarperCollins*Publishers* Ltd
77-85 Fulham Palace Road
London W6 8JB

www.**Collins**Education.com
On-line support for schools and colleges

© The Templar Company plc 1992

First published in hardback by Letterland Direct Limited 1992
This paperback edition published by Collins Educational 2000

ISBN 0 00 303477 1

LETTERLAND® is a registered trademark of Lyn Wendon.

British Library Cataloguing in Publication Data
A catalogue record for this book is available from the British Library.

Printed by
Printing Express, Hong Kong

www.**fire**and**water**.com
Visit the book lover's website